I WAS THERE

ROMAN
EMPIRE

I WAS THERE

ROMAN
EMPIRE

JOHN D. CLARE

Consultant Editor MICHAEL EDWARDS

RIVERSWIFT
LONDON

First published in Great Britain in 1992 by The Bodley Head Children's Books. This edition published 1996 by Riverswift, Random House, 20 Vauxhall Bridge Road, London SW1V 2SA.

Random House Australia Pty Ltd
20 Alfred Street, Sydney, NSW 2061, Australia

Random House New Zealand Ltd
18 Poland Road, Glenfield, Auckland 10, New Zealand

Random House South Africa Pty Ltd
PO Box 337, Bergvlei, South Africa

ISBN 1 898304 54 8

A CIP catalogue record for this book is available from the British Library

Director of Photography Tymn Lintell
Photography Charles Best
Designer Dalia Hartman
Production Manager Fiona Nicholson
Book Production Manager Ken Clark
Editor Gilly Abrahams
Series Editor Susan Elwes
Map/Time-line John Laing
Map/Time-line illustrations David Wire
Research Lesley Coleman
Typesetting Sue Estermann
Printed in China

ACKNOWLEDGEMENTS

Casting: Baba's Crew. Costume designer: Val Metheringham with Angie Woodcock, Ita Murray. Make-up: Pam Foster with Alex Vogel, Emma Scott, Michelle Bayliss, Nikita Rae. Props: Cluny South, Marissa Rossi with Eleanor Enghe. Sets: Tom Overton, Jim Dyson, Haydn Buckingham-Jones at UpSet.

Thanks also to the following: Anita Ladd, BBC Costume Dept.; Denny Edwards, Darren Finch, Bermans International and Morris Angel Ltd; Pat Perry, Tim McIlroy, Peter Reynolds and Alex Wyman, Butser Iron Age Park; The Cantina; Simon Child, Child Wilson Associates; Chislehurst Caves, Kent; Crickley Hill Archaeological Trust; Anne Hart, St Mary's Church, Clapham; Michael Harvey; Josie Heffernen; The Henson Family, Cotswold Farm Park; Fleur Kelly; Lavish Locations; Joe Lintell; Margaret Rylatt, Ed Dickinson, Coventry Archaeological Services; Jane Manning; Pandora Money; Keith Percival, National Maritime Museum, Greenwich; Road Runner Film Services; Rosemary Jury, The National Trust, Stowe Landscape Gardens; Stowe School Educational Services Ltd; Annabel James, Outright Public Relations; Mr and Mrs Shivdasani; Spink & Son Ltd, London; Pru Turnbull, John Saville, Syon Park; Dr Robert Woodward, John Woodward and the CLIC Trust; and special thanks to Chris Haines and the Ermine Street Guard.

Additional photographs: Ancient Art & Architecture Collection, P14 (centre), p16 (bottom), p39, p44 (top), p53 (top); The Austrian National Library Picture Archive, pp50-51 (main picture); C.M. Dixon, front jacket background, p14 (bottom), p20 (top, centre, bottom), p30 (top), p46 (top, bottom), p50 (top), p62 (bottom), p63; Fishbourne Roman Palace, p59 (top); The Gateway (Tyne and Wear Museums), Arbeia Roman Fort, South Shields, pp60-61; Sonia Halliday, p7, p16 (centre), pp16-17 (main picture), p44 (centre, bottom), pp48-49 (main picture), pp58-59 (main picture background), p62 (top); Museum of London, p37 (bottom).

Contents

The World of Rome

In AD 114 it was possible to travel from Scotland to the Sahara, or from Spain to Syria, and still be within the Roman Empire. Given the technology available, it was perhaps the greatest empire of all time. Almost two thousand years later, Europe is still only working towards a united government, a shared language, and a system of international law such as the Romans created.

The West still uses the Roman alphabet, Roman numerals and the Roman months. The Romans developed concrete, glass windows, the dome, central heating, blocks of flats, public health, public baths, hospitals, a postal service, a fire brigade, a civil service and international trade. Roman roads, aqueducts and buildings still survive. Latin – the language spoken by the Romans – became the basis of many European languages, including Italian, Spanish, French and English. We still use Latin words and phrases, such as et cetera (meaning 'and the rest'). Although Latin has been a 'dead' language for centuries, it is still taught in many schools.

The Birth of Rome

Archaeologists believe that Rome began, in about 1600 BC, as a collection of small round wooden huts on a group of seven hills near the River Tiber in central Italy.

In the first century BC, the Roman poet Virgil rejected such humble beginnings. His poem the *Aeneid* claimed that the Romans were the descendants of a great warrior, a Trojan prince called Aeneas. Another legend of the first century BC, told by the historian Livy, described how Rome was built by a soldier-farmer called Romulus in 753 BC. Romulus and his twin brother Remus were said to have been raised by a she-wolf – a fierce, romantic beginning for Rome.

Growing Pains

Slowly, the city grew more powerful. Its expansion was marked, not by great victories, but by frequent defeats. After each setback, however, the Romans returned to the struggle with even greater determination and slowly destroyed their enemies. During the fourth and third centuries BC, they conquered most of Italy. This brought them into conflict with the Greeks, who had settled in southern Italy. Although the Greek general Pyrrhus defeated the Romans in 279 BC, he commented: 'One more victory like this and I will be destroyed.' Soon after, he withdrew. A costly success is still called a 'pyrrhic victory'.

Contact with the Greeks, who were more cultured and educated than the Romans, had a great effect on Rome. Rich Romans bought Greek slaves to be their accountants and scribes. Most teachers and doctors were Greek. Roman literature, architecture and religion were all greatly influenced by the Greeks. Some Roman writers feared that the Romans, 'swept along on the puffs of the clever brains of the Greeks', were losing their ancient manliness and courage.

In 264 BC, Rome went to war with the city of Carthage on the north coast of Africa. After 120 years of war – including a series of disastrous defeats by the Carthaginian general Hannibal – the Romans completely destroyed Carthage in 146 BC. They ploughed salt into the fields, so nothing could ever grow there again.

The conquest of the Carthaginian Empire brought large areas of Spain and northern Africa into Rome's empire. During the second century BC, the Romans also overcame Greece and Asia Minor (modern Turkey). Some of the countries in the Empire were 'allies' – the Romans allowed their rulers to stay in power as long as they paid taxes to Rome. Conquered countries, however, were divided into provinces and ruled by Roman governors.

Government and Society

In 509 BC the Romans expelled the last of their kings. Rome became a republic. Its citizens were free men and believed that they had the right and duty to run the government. Each year they elected two consuls, who ran the city's affairs for the next year and served as generals in times of war. Other government officials were also elected. When their period of office was over, they became life members of the Senate – the parliament of the Roman Empire. As senators were not paid, most came from the nobility, who had acquired large estates and great wealth.

The Senate ran the government of Rome. It advised the consuls. Political problems were discussed in the Senate. Citizens could vote to accept or reject new laws in their assemblies.

A bright young man from a rich family would serve in the army until his late twenties, when he would stand for election as a quaestor. If elected, he gained entry to the Senate and would help to run the state treasury. Later, he might become an aedile (in charge of police work, public health or the public games), or a tribune (elected to safeguard the rights of the plebeians – the ordinary people). In his late thirties he would stand for election as a praetor (judge and general), and in his early forties as one of the two consuls. He would hope to be appointed by the Senate as a provincial governor.

Many of the leading families were known as patricians. Everybody who was not a patrician was a plebeian. Some plebeians, such as the bankers, factory owners and merchants, were very rich. Others were farmers, shopkeepers, labourers or fortune-tellers. Although the nobles despised trade as 'degrading and vulgar', there were vast numbers of goldsmiths, cobblers, girdle-makers and other traders in Rome. Many of these men were very poor but they were still Roman citizens and had the right to vote in elections. Freemen (who had been born free) counted themselves better than freedmen (slaves who had been granted their freedom). Women, however highborn, were not citizens and had few legal rights. They were dependent on their fathers or husbands and could not vote. In some respects they were little better off than the slaves, who were dependent on their masters and also had no vote.

Time and Money

The Romans divided the year into 12 months. They numbered the days, however, by their distance before or after three key days within each month: the calends (the first day of the month); the nones (the fifth, or the seventh day in March, May, July and October – the so-called 'long' months); and the ides (the thirteenth, or the fifteenth day in the long months). The hours of daylight were split into 12 equal periods; in this way, an 'hour' was longer in summer than in winter.

A small bronze quadrans was the usual entrance fee to the baths (see page 34). There were four quadrantes in an as (another bronze coin), four asses in a sesterce (a small silver coin), and four sesterces in a silver denarius, the craftsman's daily wage.

Left: rich young Romans enjoy the dangers and excitement of a boar hunt.

The Roman Army

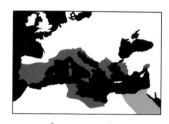

For a thousand years, from the fifth century BC to the fifth century AD, the Romans were continually at war. Their army became the most efficient in the world.

In the second century BC, the army was made up of four legions. Each legion comprised about five thousand legionaries. The consul or praetor in charge of the legion was helped by a *legatus*, who was also a senator, and by six young noblemen called military tribunes. The basic unit was a group of men called a century, because it had originally comprised about one hundred men. It was commanded by a professional soldier called a centurion. Later, each century was divided into *contubernia*, groups of eight men who shared a tent, a mule and a millstone.

At the beginning of each year, the two consuls called all the land-owning citizens between the ages of 17 and 46 to the Capitoline Hill overlooking Rome. Here the military tribunes chose the strongest men for the army. The men did not serve full time, but were called up when they were needed for a specific campaign.

In an age when most battles consisted of a single wild charge, after which one side or the other turned and fled, the greatest strength of the Roman soldiers was their discipline. Roman generals, said the Greek writer Polybius, wanted men 'who will hold their ground when outnumbered and hard pressed and who will die at their posts'. The soldiers fought in line, about 1.2 metres (4 feet) apart. First, they threw their *pila* (javelins). Then they drew their swords, protecting themselves with their shields. As the men in the front row fell, soldiers from the row behind stepped into their places.

A company that retreated was decimated – every tenth man was taken out and beaten to death with wooden clubs. Brave soldiers, on the other hand, were given rewards. An infantryman who killed an enemy soldier in single combat received a drinking bowl. The first man to climb the wall of a besieged city won a gold crown. As a result, Polybius warned, 'it is inevitable that the outcome of every war the Romans fight is brilliantly successful'.

In 107 BC, the consul Gaius Marius realized that Rome needed a professional, permanent army. He changed the rules for enlistment, allowing men without land to join the army as a career. By the first century AD, soldiers signed up for 16 to 20 years. At the end of their service they were given money or some land to farm. When not fighting or training, soldiers were used to build roads, bridges and aqueducts (see pages 48-50).

Roman soldiers practise their fighting skills. The secret of the Roman Army's success, writes Josephus, the Jewish historian, is its training – 'as fierce as a real war' – and the men's absolute obedience to their officers.

Left: a senator and officers of the Roman Army in the first century AD. Left to right: a *signifer*, carrying the standard of a century; an *aquilifer*, carrying the eagle of the legion; a *signifer* carrying a *vexillum* (flag); a centurion; and a *cornicen* (horn blower).

The map shows the Empire in about 100 BC.

The Death of the Republic

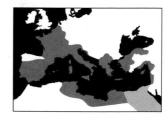

In the first century BC, things began to go wrong in the Republic. Politicians became corrupt, building up large numbers of supporters (called clients) by giving them money and doing them favours. There was cut-throat competition for jobs in the government. As a result, the number of senators rose rapidly – by 44 BC there were more than a thousand.

The Senate began to lose control of the Empire. The cities of Italy rebelled. Two army generals – Marius (see page 8) and Cornelius Sulla – became involved in a struggle for power. In 87 BC Marius's men marched through the streets of Rome, killing anybody he pointed out. Four years later Sulla entered Rome, drew up lists of Marius's supporters and set out to slaughter them. Hundreds of

citizens were beheaded and their heads nailed up in the centre of Rome.

In 73 BC there was a slave revolt, led by Spartacus, a gladiator (see page 44). For two years, seventy thousand slaves rampaged through southern Italy. It took an army of eight legions to defeat them; two legions were decimated for cowardice. Six thousand slaves were crucified and left to rot along the Appian Way, the main road from Rome to the south.

In 49 BC Julius Caesar seized control of the Empire. Caesar was a successful general who, in the years 58-51 BC, had conquered Gaul (France) and invaded Britain. He led his forces across the Rubicon, the stream that separated Italy from Gaul, and marched into Rome.

On the ides of March, 44 BC, a group of assassins led by the senator Cassius, murder Caesar in the Senate because they suspect that he is planning to make himself king. One of the men, Brutus, is Caesar's friend. Seeing him amongst the attackers, Caesar calls out sorrowfully, 'Et tu, Brute!' ('You too, Brutus!')

The map shows the extent of the Empire in 44 BC.

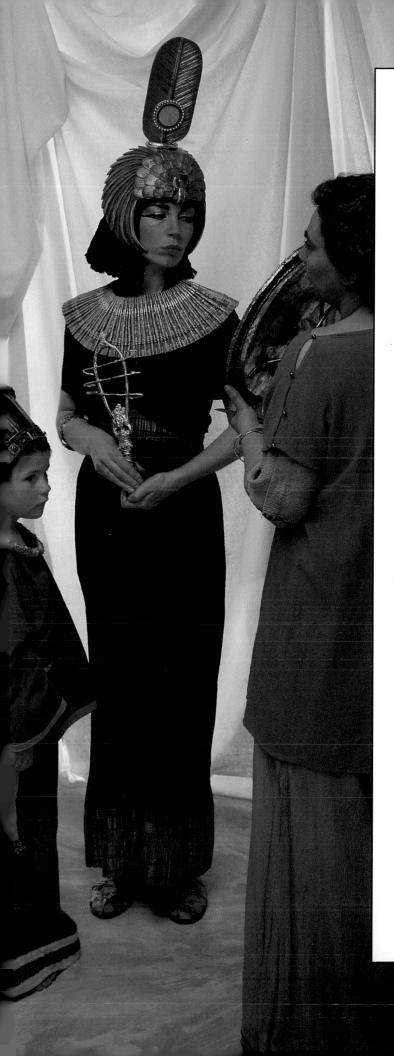

The Rivals

After the assassination of Julius Caesar, his friend and ally, Mark Antony, gained control of the Senate by murdering three hundred senators. Caesar was declared to be a god (see page 18). Brutus and Cassius fled with an army to Greece.

Antony was supported by Caesar's great-nephew, Octavian, a young general. According to Suetonius, an historian who loved to include gory details even if they were only gossip, Octavian defeated Brutus and sent his head to Rome, leaving the rebels' bodies to rot in the fields. On 15 March 41 BC, he sacrificed three hundred prisoners to the god Julius.

For a time, Antony and Octavian ruled jointly, Octavian in western Europe and Antony in Egypt, at that time the richest country in the Empire. In Rome, Octavian made friends with the Senate and became a consul. In Egypt, Antony fell in love with Cleopatra, the Queen of Egypt.

We cannot know what Cleopatra was really like, because the Roman historians hated her. Even long afterwards, the writer Plutarch presented her as a beautiful and wicked enchantress, who lay under a golden canopy, fanned by handsome young boys, her maids dressed as nymphs. She believed she was destined to rule the world.

Rapidly, Octavian and Antony became rivals. In 31 BC Octavian's navy destroyed Antony's forces at the sea-battle of Actium. Antony committed suicide by falling on his sword. Cleopatra was captured but later killed herself, using a poisonous snake which her maids had smuggled into her room.

Antony and Cleopatra prepare to present their children to the Egyptian people, in a spectacle designed to display their power. Their daughter (centre) is dressed in the costume of Libya, their sons as the kings of Persia (right) and Greece (left). Cleopatra is dressed as the Egyptian goddess Isis.

The Empire under Augustus

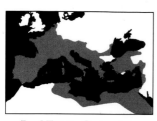

After he had defeated Antony and Cleopatra, Octavian secured his power over the Empire – by giving it away!

In 27 BC, Octavian announced his plans for the Empire. Although he accepted the title 'Augustus' (meaning dignified), he refused offers to become king. The Senate, he said, would rule Italy and those parts of the Empire that were 'peaceful and easy to govern'. He offered to take the imperium (supreme power) in Egypt, and in the provinces 'that are restless and rebellious': Spain, Gaul and Syria.

This was very clever of Augustus. He could claim to have saved the Senate and the Republic from the rebels. Now, he seemed to be taking all the problems of government upon himself. The Senate happily agreed to Augustus's plan.

The areas where there was a danger of rebellion, however, were the areas where the army was stationed; Augustus had given himself control of 22 of the 25 Roman legions. Also, although officially there were no legions stationed in Italy, Augustus made sure that he had armed forces near Rome. He enlarged his bodyguard – the Praetorian Guard – to 4,500 men. He also took control of three units of soldiers who acted as the city

police, and of the *vigiles*, the soldiers who served as Rome's fire brigade. They were not very skilled fire-fighters. Nicknamed the 'little bucket fellows', they were famous for mistakenly bursting in on barbecues and soaking the guests. There were, however, seven thousand *vigiles*, and it is clear that they were meant to be more than firemen. With the Praetorian Guard, the *vigiles* and the police, Augustus had thirteen thousand soldiers under his command in the city of Rome.

Augustus never needed to use these legions. Egypt was the richest province in the Empire, and the money it provided allowed Augustus to build up a huge following of clients. A hint from Augustus was usually enough to make sure that all the senators voted the way he wanted.

The new government was a fraud. It kept all the appearances of the old republic, but one man had total control. Augustus was an autocrat (sole ruler), but his rule was a *disguised* autocracy.

Shortly before he died in AD 14, at the age of 76, Augustus wrote the *Res Gestae* – an account of his reign and achievements, 'whereby he brought the whole world under the rule of the Roman people'. He claimed that he had 'raised an army and set the Republic free'. He had provided Rome with grain and had made gifts of money to the people and the soldiers. He had built many fine buildings in Rome (see page 46) and restored 82 temples. He had organized many public entertainments, including eight contests of gladiators (involving a total of ten thousand men), 27 public games, and 26 public spectacles of wild beasts, in which 3,500 animals died.

Augustus is sometimes called 'the second founder of Rome'. He introduced the idea of using auxiliaries in the Roman army: in each province he enlisted native soldiers who were paid less than the legionaries, but were given Roman citizenship when they had finished their term of service. He attacked the barbarians in the north of Europe, reaching the easily defendable frontiers of the River Danube and the River Rhine. At the same time, he disbanded many legions and concentrated on giving the Empire good government. Trade increased and the people prospered.

For the next five centuries the Empire was ruled by emperors. Augustus's reign was the start of the *Pax Romana*, the 'Roman peace'. Looking back in AD 38, the Jewish Egyptian scholar Philo commented that 'the whole human race would have been destroyed, had it not been for one man, Augustus…who ended wars…set every city at liberty…civilized all the unfriendly, savage tribes…and safeguarded peace….'

The historian Tacitus was less enthusiastic. Writing in about AD 110, he described how Augustus 'tricked the army by giving them gifts, the common people by giving them cheap food, and everyone by peace, then little by little he began to increase his powers, to steal the authority of the Senate, the magistrates and the laws… So the state had been changed, and the old, free Roman people no longer existed'.

Augustus (right) always speaks first in the Senate, so the senators know how they have to vote. He boasts that he also controls his third wife, Livia (above left), but she openly acts and dresses as she pleases. Far left: the imperial family with members of the Senate.

The map shows the extent of the Empire in AD 14.

Farming and Superstition

Most people lived in the countryside and worked on the land. Rich Romans gained their income from farming and preferred their country estates to the crowded towns. Roman writers praised rural values, comparing the 'soft' city-dwellers of Rome with the tough farmers, 'who knew how to turn the earth with hoes, and to chop and carry in firewood until evening'.

The pagans (from the Latin word *pagani*, meaning 'country folk') believed that every place had its numen (guardian spirit), which must not be offended. Over the centuries, certain spirits became more important than others – for instance, all Romans worshipped Jupiter, the weather spirit – but country life remained full of religious rituals to please the spirits. Before a farmer could thin out a copse of trees, for example, he had first to sacrifice a pig and say prayers.

Roman religion developed from the primitive spirit-worship of the farmers. In the Temple of Mars, the priests performed a strange dance, chanting: 'Be filled, fierce Mars. Leap over the doorstep. Stop, wild one. Call on the gods of the seed.' At the word 'leap', they all jumped into the air. Mars had been the spirit of farming and the priests were reciting an ancient farming prayer. The leap symbolized the growth of the crops.

The Romans were very superstitious. There were, they believed, a number of *dies nefasti* (unlucky days); the Senate did not meet and no business was done on these days. The left side of anything was also unlucky: our word 'sinister' is the Latin word for 'left'. Augustus never put on his left shoe first.

Many Romans honour the gods. The hunters (right) offer sacrifices to Diana, the goddess of hunting – 'queen of the green forests, trackless glens and murmuring streams' – before they set out.

Top left: each year, on 23 February, Terminus (the god of the boundary markers) is honoured. At dawn, the boundary stone between two farms is crowned with a garland. The farmer builds a fire on which he will burn offerings such as sliced honeycombs and a sacrificial piglet.

Although farmers in Gaul have invented a reaping machine (left), most farming is done by labourers using hand-tools (centre left). The soil of Italy is fertile and the climate is favourable, so crops grow well.

Gods and Religion

Early in their history, the Romans decided that the spirits they worshipped were the same as the gods of the Greeks. Jupiter, for instance, was Zeus, king of the gods; Mars was Ares, the god of war. Over the centuries they adopted the gods of the countries they had conquered. Also, most Roman emperors were declared to be gods after their death.

The Romans took care not to offend the gods. They consulted augurs (who predicted the gods' wishes from the behaviour of birds) and haruspices (who examined the livers of sacrificed animals to see if the omens were favourable). A Roman would not travel, get married, or fight a battle if the sacred chickens were not eating. The Roman Army even offered sacrifices to their enemies' gods, trying to persuade them to support the Romans instead.

When Augustus was emperor, there were 66 religious festivals. The most important was the Saturnalia (17-20 December), a time of eating, drinking and giving presents. At the Lupercalia (15 February) young men, covered in blood, ran round naked and howling, perhaps in memory of the she-wolf that had suckled Romulus and Remus.

'This is the religion that made the whole world obey us,' a Roman wrote in AD 384, but even by the time of Augustus, many educated Romans did not believe in the gods.

To please the gods, the Romans build temples and conduct sacrifices. The priest, his head covered with his toga, throws incense onto the altar, while attendants bring wine, fruit and a lamb. They believe that prayers are granted only if they are said in exactly the right way, so while one man reads the prayer out loud, another checks that he is doing it correctly, and a third plays a flute to drown out any other noises!

Romans do not attend the temples regularly. They worship the gods only when they want something. A young man might ask Venus, the goddess of love, to give him the opportunity to kiss his girlfriend. The priests might ask Jupiter for victory in a war.

Trade and Traders

Throughout the Empire, everybody lived under Roman law and most people could speak Latin. As a result, trade flourished. Rome, said the Greek writer Aristides, was 'a common market for the world'.

Goods were usually sent by sea. It cost as much to transport grain 50 miles (80 kilometres) by road as it did to take it 1,250 miles (2,000 kilometres) by sea, and merchant ships could sail from Rome to Egypt in less than a fortnight.

Many of the imports which came into the city of Rome were tribute or taxes from the provinces. The port of Ostia, the harbour at the mouth of the River Tiber, 15 miles (25 kilometres) from Rome, was full of government officials checking deliveries, supervising loading and paying crews. From Spain came wine, olive oil, honey, salt fish, wax, pitch, a red dye made from crushed beetles, black wool and fine cloth. There were also wines from France, glassware and cloth from Syria, shoes from Greece, incense from Arabia and marble from Africa and Asia. In addition, the Romans imported Baltic amber, Babylonian robes, gems from India and silks from the Far East.

The most important trade was in grain; without large imports the people of Rome

would have starved. Every year more than 400,000 tons of grain from Africa, Egypt and Sicily passed through Ostia and the port of Puteoli, near Naples, on its way to Rome.

The merchants and tradesmen formed *collegia* (social clubs), where they met each month to feast and to worship their genius (patron spirit). Gravestones in Ostia record *collegia* of shipowners, grain merchants, wine dealers, warehousemen and bargees, as well as shipbuilders, caulkers (who waterproofed the ships) and ballast men.

Top: scribes record the number of amphorae (large clay jars) being unloaded from a merchant ship. The ship's rigging can be seen in the background. Cargoes unloaded at Ostia are put on barges (above) and towed, sometimes by slaves, up the River Tiber to Rome.

Amphorae that have contained olive oil cannot be reused as the oil soaks into the pottery and goes rancid, so the empty pots are smashed (right), to be used as ballast on the ship's homeward journey.

Left: there is an extensive trade in fine glassware.

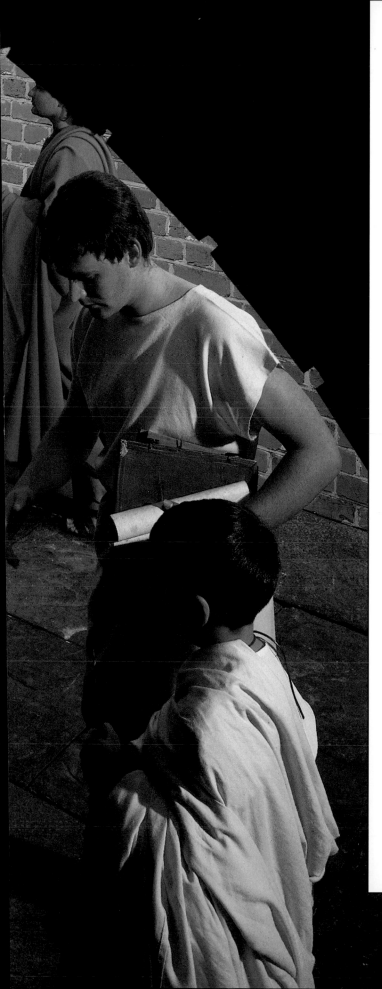

The Streets of Rome

Although there were towns before the Romans, it was the Romans who developed urban living as a way of life. Our word civilization comes from *civitas*, the Latin word for town.

More than a million people lived in Rome. Before large areas were destroyed by fire in AD 64 (see page 46), the city was a maze of busy, narrow streets. 'However fast you hurry there's a huge crowd ahead and a mob behind, pushing and shoving,' complained the writer Juvenal in the first century AD. 'The streets are filthy – our legs are plastered with mud – and you are sure to get a soldier's great hobnailed boot on your toe....'

Julius Caesar had tried to reduce the congestion by ordering shopkeepers to move their wagons only at night, but builders' carts, rubbish carts and religious vehicles were exempt, so the law made little difference during the day, and everyone was kept awake at night. 'There's nowhere a man can get any peace in Rome,' complained the poet Martial. 'Shouting schoolmasters wake you up at the crack of dawn, at night it's the bakers, and all day long it's the coppersmiths with their hammers. There's a never-ending stream of noisy soldiers, shipwrecked sailors covered in bandages, and Jewish beggars.'

Graffiti scratched on the walls proclaimed: 'Don't pee here, the stinging nettles are tall'; 'Iris only loves Successus because she feels sorry for him'; '65 sesterces to anyone who brings back my copper pot'. The smell of food from the hot-food sellers mingled with the stink of rubbish thrown into the road. Juvenal warned: 'Each open window may be a death-trap – so hope and pray, you poor man, that the local housewife drops nothing worse on your head than a bucket of slops!'

A wealthy woman is carried on a litter past a lamp shop, and a slave takes a boy home from school.

The Forum

Every Roman town had a forum, an open space where people met, but the Forum Romanum in Rome was the most famous. Every milestone on every road in Italy recorded its distance from a marker set up in the Forum, hence the saying, 'All roads lead to Rome'.

Around the Forum were the law courts, the Senate House and the offices of the merchants and bankers. There were also a number of temples, including the Temple of Vesta, the goddess of the hearth (the centre of family life). Occasionally, the Roman people met here to worship at the Eternal Flame which burned on the altar.

The Forum was always full of bustling activity. It was a market-place. The sundial (brought to Rome in 263 BC) was set in the Forum, to divide the daylight into 12 equal 'hours' of business.

At about the third hour the rich politicians wandered down to the Forum from their houses on the Palatine Hill, maybe to go to the Senate House, or to speak from the rostra – a speakers' platform built from the *rostra* (prows) of captured enemy ships.

Eventually the Forum became so crowded that no one could move. Augustus tried to solve this by completing the Forum of Julius (started by Julius Caesar) and building the Forum of Augustus nearby.

A senator (left), wearing a toga with a broad, purple stripe, is going to the basilica (public building) to defend one of his clients in the law courts. A woman reads her poems to a small group of friends and her husband's clients. A boy who has reached the age of 16 exchanges his childhood toga with its purple stripe for a white *toga virilis* (toga of manhood), given to him by his father. Behind, a funeral procession stops to hear a panegyric, a speech in praise of the dead person. Tourists have come to see the tomb of Romulus. Other people discuss the items in the handwritten newspaper, the *Acta Diurna* (Daily Events).

25

A Wealthy Wife

The Romans believed that women were the weaker sex. Doctors thought that a woman's womb moved about inside her body (from her stomach to her legs) causing hysteria, fainting and fits. Families mourned when a girl was born, and it is common to read of daughters who were hated by their fathers. Sometimes a father would leave a baby girl out in the cold to die.

Highborn girls were expected to marry and have children. A tombstone records the short, sad life of a woman called Veturia: 'My father was Veturius. My husband was Fortunatus. I lived 27 years, and I was married for 16 years to the same man. After giving birth to six children, only one of whom lived, I died.'

'Hard work, lack of sleep, hands rough from working wool' – these were the signs of a good wife. She was supposed to look after the household, support her husband, and be quiet, loving and obedient. When one man hesitated after being ordered to commit suicide, his wife stabbed herself to give him courage. 'It does not hurt,' she assured him.

After the time of Augustus, the position of women improved a little. A few educated women became teachers and doctors. Some, such as Eumachia who owned a brickyard in Pompeii, ran successful businesses. Wealthy women discussed poetry, law and literature, and tried to influence politics by dominating their husbands.

A rich Roman lady, says Martial, keeps her beauty in a hundred boxes. Her slaves have rubbed a mixture made from rats' heads, rats' dung and pepper into her hair to try to prevent baldness, and she has used a face-pack made of bread and cream. She puts in false teeth (imported from Germany), sucks sweets to freshen her breath, plucks her eyebrows, wears jewellery and uses powder, rouge and scent.

Above: she puts on a *stola* (dress) and *palla* (cloak).
Below: a slave dresses her husband in his toga.

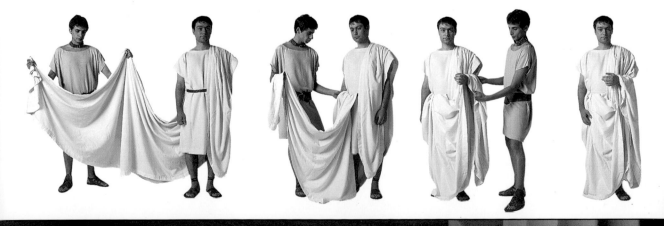

Morning Callers

Some rich Romans lived in palatial mansions, decorated with mosaics, wall-paintings and intricately patterned marble floors. Their elegant furniture was made of ivory, bronze and fine wood.

In such households the man rose, washed and shaved before dawn. Pious parents would pray for the family and the emperor at the *lararium* (household shrine). The wet-nurse fed the baby. Children were often strictly disciplined and were expected to be seen and not heard. Girls did their hair and perhaps played quietly with a pet monkey while they waited for their Greek tutor to arrive. Boys kissed their parents goodbye and, accompanied by a slave, left for school while it was still dark, buying something to eat from the baker's on the way. Sometimes, but not always, the family breakfasted on bread and cheese.

A rich Roman would then open his doors

to a queue of callers – his clients. These poor men depended on the six sesterces a day (or its equivalent in bread) which he gave them. In return, they visited their patron every day, provided an escort for him in the street, accompanied him to the baths and swelled the audience when he gave a public reading of his poetry.

Having greeted these callers, the rich Roman would set off to the law courts, or perhaps the Senate. Later in the morning, he would deal with business matters. At midday – after, in summer, perhaps seven or eight hours' work – he might have a light *prandium* (lunch) of bread, cheese, olives, figs and nuts, followed by a siesta (rest).

These clients (above) have hurried across Rome in the rain to say 'Good morning, my Lord,' to their patron. They are divided into two rows: 'first-class' friends stand in front of the general public. The patron (above left) is more interested in his career. He ignores most of them, greets the others with a tired yawn and slips out with a slave to salute his own patron.

'*Festina lente!*' ('Take it easy!') cries the parrot.

Insulae

A survey of Rome in AD 350 showed that there were only 1,782 private houses. Most people lived in rented accommodation in one of the 46,602 blocks of flats, called *insulae* ('islands'). A typical *insula* was up to six storeys high, with shops on the ground floor, and was bounded on all sides by streets.

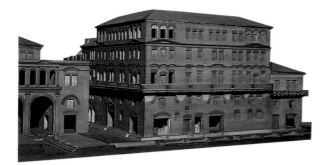

In Rome, the rich and the poor lived side by side. A wealthy family might pay 30,000 sesterces a year for a large penthouse. Most *insulae*, however, were not so grand and were the homes of the poorer plebeians – the fruit-sellers and fishmongers, butchers and bath attendants, polishers and porters who formed the bulk of the population of Rome. In this layer of society women worked as the equals of men; inscriptions on their tombstones tell us that they also worked as midwives, dress-makers and mime artists.

Rents in Rome were very expensive – 2,000 sesterces a year even for a tiny flat – but most *insulae* were badly built and poorly maintained. The mud-and-wattle walls dried out in summer, cracking and crumbling. Few of the plebeians' rooms had any heating apart from, perhaps, a charcoal brazier. The very poor had nothing to cook on; they had to eat cold food, or buy hot snacks from the taverns and hot-food shops. Water had to be carried up from the public fountains. A few *insulae* had a shared lavatory in the basement – otherwise people had to use the public latrines (see page 49). In winter, with the shutters closed to keep out the cold, the air in the *insulae* became stale; sometimes poor people burned bread to overcome the smell.

'The simple life of the poor involves suffering every day – a pot with a broken handle, a fireplace without a fire, a beggar's rug, an old camp bed riddled with bed bugs and a toga that's too short and worn night and day,' writes Martial in the first century AD.

Above left: an *insula* in Ostia, the port of Rome, with a warehouse on the ground floor.

Slaves

Romans were judged by the number of their slaves (one senator had 4,116) and liked to boast that they did nothing for themselves. One rich man even asked his slaves: 'Am I seated?' He employed them to worry about such things.

Most slaves had been criminals or prisoners of war; Julius Caesar brought back one million men, women and children from Gaul. All slaves' children were born into slavery. They were branded, or wore a collar which bore the message: 'I have escaped. Send me back to my master.'

Slavery was accepted as normal. An educated slave would borrow money from his master, buy a boy and train him, then sell him to the master at a profit. Some masters loved their slaves, and even sent them on holiday to Egypt if they were sick. Rome was full of 'lazy, sleepy slaves, lounging around waiting for their masters at the playing field, or the theatres, betting shops and snack bars'. Farm work was harder. City masters threatened their slaves: 'I'll send you to work on the farm!'

Slavery became vital to the Roman economy. The city government had its own slaves, who were used as builders and street sweepers. Slaves formed the workforce of the factories and the silver mines, where they 'pray for death, so great is their suffering'. When the slaves of gladiator trainers were too old to fight, they were thrown to the lions.

After the slave revolt of 73 BC (see page 11), many Romans feared the slaves. Seneca, a Roman politician, tells us that it was once proposed in the Senate to make all slaves wear special clothes – until someone pointed out that they would then be able to see that they outnumbered their masters. They were often brutally punished for small mistakes. One man used to throw them into his fishpond and watch as they were torn apart by huge, eel-like lampreys. If a slave killed his master, all the slaves in the household were executed.

Above left: a good slave can be bought for 2,000 denarii, although a pretty girl might cost 50,000, including tax. The sales contract states that they are 'non-returnable, except for epilepsy'.

Above: an intelligent young slave saves the *peculia* (money gifts) given to him by his satisfied master and after many years is able to buy his freedom in a special ceremony.

Right, top to bottom: slaves do menial tasks and work as cooks, nurses and masseurs in rich households. Educated slaves (often Greeks) are much in demand as doctors and accountants.

The Baths

In the afternoon many Romans went to the public baths. In the reign of Augustus there were about 170 bathhouses in Rome, and by AD 300 the number had risen to more than nine hundred. The largest, the Baths of Diocletian completed in AD 305, were as high as St Paul's Cathedral in London, with eight times the floor area – space for three thousand bathers. Some baths were incredibly luxurious: 'We think ourselves badly done to if the walls are not covered in mirrors, the ceilings are not buried in glass and the pools lined with marble,' wrote Seneca.

Most baths had a number of different rooms. A bather would start in the *tepidarium* (warm pool), move from there into the *caldarium* (hot pool), then go to the *frigidarium* (cold pool). Many baths also had a *Laconicum* (extra hot, for invalids), a gymnasium, gardens, a library reading room and snack bars.

For a quadrans any Roman could go to the bathhouse to wash, swim, jog, wrestle – or just gossip; the baths were places to meet friends and conduct business. Hack poets recited their verses and hoped for an invitation to dinner. Muscle-men showed off their weight-lifting. Seneca, who lived above a bathhouse, complained about the noise: '…the man who likes to sing in the bath; men who jump into the water with an almighty splash; and then the cries of "Cakes for sale" and "Hot sausages".' Sometimes a rich Roman, as an act of charity, would pay everybody's entrance fees for a whole day.

Strict Romans such as Seneca thought the baths were a sign of a deterioration in the Roman character, and looked back to the 'good old days' when men washed once a week and smelt of the farm and the army.

In a small suburban bathhouse one bather is massaged, while another has oiled himself (the Romans do not have soap) and is scraping away the dirt with a *strigil*.

An Evening Meal

The *cena* (main meal of the day) usually took place in the evening. It was held in an upper room of the house, called the *triclinium* after the couches on which the diners reclined. Not every *cena* was a feast. Most meals were 'humble little dinners' of fresh vegetables, sausage in semolina, bacon and beans. Poor people had to make do, day after day, with porridge made from bread boiled in water, and served in earthenware bowls.

Wealthy Romans, however, seem to have loved to eat to excess. Food was rich and elaborate. An appetizer course – usually raw vegetables, eggs and fish – would be served.

The main course might include stuffed dormice, teats from a sow's udder, or lamb's womb stuffed with sausage meat. The feast given by Trimalchio, a character in a Roman novel, included a wild boar stuffed with live thrushes, which flew out when the meat was carved but were then caught and cooked. Desserts were usually fresh or dried fruit, seasoned with pepper to bring out the coolness of the fruit. When they were full, guests sometimes made themselves sick to make room for more food.

A good host would hire singers, dancing girls or a comic turn. 'I won't read you my poetry,' promised Martial, but most guests had to listen to their host's latest verses.

Politics was far too dangerous a topic of

conversation. Romans discussed issues such as the Greens and the Blues (see page 44), whether smoking dried cow-dung through a reed really cured tuberculosis, or how rubbing hares' brains on a baby's gums stopped teething pains. All Romans were touchy about their position in society. If a freedman felt he was being mocked, he would lose his temper: 'I was a slave for 40 years. I worked hard and made my way successfully. So what are you staring at, you smelly goat?'

Less wealthy guests wrapped leftover food in their napkins, to sell the next day. Drunkenness and bad behaviour were common. In Pompeii, one host wrote his house rules on the wall: 'Be friendly and don't quarrel. If you can't, go home.'

These wealthy Romans recline on couches while they dine. Slaves stand by to offer more food and drink, and to clear up the mess; the diners throw bones and scraps on the floor.

Below: in most houses the kitchen is a small room with a raised hearth, on top of which a wood or charcoal fire is lit. Fuel is stored underneath. The food is grilled, or boiled in bronze pots placed on a metal stand.

After Augustus

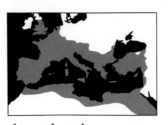

Many Roman historians yearned for the 'good old days' of the Republic, and openly admitted they were trying to show that the emperors were wicked. As a result, it is difficult to know what is true and what the historians invented when they wrote their accounts of the emperors who followed Augustus.

Tiberius Claudius Nero, AD 14-37

Tiberius, who had been nominated by Augustus as his successor, became emperor in AD 14. The historian Suetonius tells us that he was a large man with pimples, and that his forefinger was so strong that he could push it through a ripe apple. Tiberius hated crowds and was scared of thunder. In private, Romans called him Biberius Caldius Mero, which means 'drunk, wine-drowned boozer' – a comic reference to his name. When he died, people ran about joyfully, shouting: 'Throw Tiberius in the Tiber!'

Tiberius continued Augustus's policies of peace and disguised autocracy. He refused the title of *imperator*, saying that he wanted senators to speak and vote freely. At the same time, he made it treason to say or write anything hostile about him. Consequently, none of the senators dared to reveal their true opinions. One openly asked Tiberius to vote before him in the Senate. 'Then I can follow your lead; otherwise, I fear that I may vote against you,' he told the Emperor. 'This was a rotten, pitiful age of yes-men,' commented the historian Tacitus.

During the reign of Tiberius a Jewish preacher called Joshua ben Joseph, known as

Jesus the Christ, was put to death in Jerusalem by the Roman governor, Pontius Pilate.

Gaius, AD 37-41

Gaius was nicknamed Caligula after the tiny soldier's boots (*caligae*) he wore as a child. When he became emperor he threw a banquet for all the wealthiest people, gave every citizen three gold coins and added a fifth day to the Saturnalia holiday. Suetonius tells us that people thought their dreams had come true. To thank the gods, 160,000 animals were sacrificed in three months. 'So much for Gaius the Emperor,' adds Suetonius. 'The rest of my history must deal with Gaius the monster.'

Gaius abandoned the policy of disguised power and ruled openly as an autocrat. He even claimed to be a god. Dozens of people were murdered or executed for treason. The Roman historians hated him; they tell outrageous stories about how he made the legions collect seashells, and proposed his favourite horse as a senator. We will never know whether Caligula was mad, bad, or just a failed tyrant who was libelled by those who opposed him.

On 24 January 41, Caligula was murdered by the Praetorian Guards. If Suetonius is to be trusted, people refused to believe he was dead, thinking it was a trick to discover what they would say. The story would have amused Caligula, who used to practise making faces in front of the mirror so that he could frighten people.

Claudius, AD 41-54

Claudius was tall and handsome but he stammered, dribbled and twitched. Suetonius tells us that his mother called him 'a monster', and quotes a letter written by Augustus, ordering that he was not to be seen in public because people would laugh. Instead,

Claudius studied history and wrote books.

He was a clever and popular emperor, although on one occasion, when grain supplies ran low, he was attacked in the streets by an angry mob. Claudius decreed that slaves should not be abandoned or put to death by their owners when they became old or sick. He ruled with the help of a council of ministers, including a secretary, a chancellor and a financial adviser. He encouraged the senators who disagreed with him to speak out, and he was the first emperor to invite citizens from the provinces to become senators. During his reign Britain was conquered (AD 43), and Claudius went in person to receive the surrender of the eleven British kings.

Claudius was murdered in AD 54 by his fourth wife (his niece Agrippina), who wanted her son Nero to become emperor.

After Caligula's assassination, the Praetorian soldiers (below), realizing that without an emperor to guard they will be out of a job, search through the palace for a suitable successor. Claudius is discovered hiding behind a curtain and is proclaimed emperor.

The map shows the extent of the Roman Empire at the time of Claudius's death.

Christianity

Few educated Romans believed in the old gods of the state religion, which was concerned mainly with formal rituals. Some, wanting a personal religion, began to worship foreign gods, such as the Persian god Mithras, the Egyptian goddess Isis and the Greek god Bacchus. Ordinary Romans were suspicious of these religions. The Bacchants, who used wine in their worship, were accused of having drunken orgies; their religion was eventually forbidden. Christianity, wrote Tacitus, was just another of these 'hideous and shameful' religions from the East, which Romans began to adopt.

Nero, who became emperor after Claudius, persecuted the Christians, accusing them of starting the Great Fire of Rome in AD 64. On Nero's orders, some had animal skins tied around them, then they were attacked by dogs who tore them apart. Others were coated with tar and crucified on stakes in Nero's garden. When it grew dark, they were set on fire to provide light for Nero's parties. The Emperor's extreme cruelty merely made people feel sorry for the Christians, 'even though they were guilty and deserved to die', Tacitus wrote.

Over the years, Christians were often persecuted by the emperors. Nevertheless, the religion spread steadily. In the reign of the Emperor Constantine (AD 306-337), it became the official religion of the Roman Empire.

The police raid a Christian meeting which is being held secretly in the catacombs, the old underground burial chambers in Rome.

In their Eucharist (thankful) meals the Christians share bread and wine, 'the body and blood' of Christ, so they are accused of cannibalism. They refuse to make sacrifices to the emperor because they worship only one god, so they are accused of treason. Most Christians share their possessions, and many are poor people and slaves, so it is said they are plotting a revolution to overthrow the rich.

Famous Last Words

If Tacitus and Suetonius are to be believed, Nero was interested only in music, riding and disgusting orgies. He performed in public as an actor and singer, wearing nothing but a dressing-gown, slippers and a scarf. During these appearances the doors of the theatre were locked and soldiers of the Praetorian Guard patrolled the crowd, hitting those who were not cheering. Some members of the audience pretended to have heart attacks so they could be carried out. For two years (AD 66-68) Nero toured Greece, winning prizes in the Olympic Games for acting, lute-playing and chariot-racing – even though he fell out of his chariot. The Greeks genuinely liked him, calling him 'the new Apollo' (the Greek sun god).

In Rome, however, old-fashioned Romans were angry that their emperor was acting in public and that he was mixing with Greeks. A string of plots was hatched against him, and the number of executions and forced suicides grew. Nero had both his mother and his wife murdered. One man was exiled because he was called Cassius, the name of one of Caesar's murderers (see page 11). In AD 65, after the discovery of a plot led by a nobleman called Piso, the politician Seneca was one of more than 20 leading citizens sentenced to death. He chose suicide, rather than the humiliation of a public execution.

Nero also began to lose control of the provinces of the Empire, perhaps because of slack government, or because he was trying to reduce the powers of the provincial governors. There was a revolt in Britain, led by Boudicca, the Queen of the Iceni tribe. The Jews of Palestina (Judaea) rebelled. The German legions grew mutinous.

Finally, in AD 68, Vindex, the governor of Gaul, revolted. Although he had no army, he was supported by the governor of Spain, Sulpicius Galba. Nero panicked, and in June tried to flee to Egypt. That night the Praetorian Guard deserted, after a bribe from Galba's supporters of 7,500 denarii for each man. The Senate declared the Emperor a public enemy and sentenced him to be flogged to death. Nero committed suicide, stabbing himself in

Galba, AD 68-69

Nero, AD 54-68

Otho, AD 69

the throat with a dagger. His last words were: 'What a showman the world is losing!'

AD 69 and After

AD 69 was the 'year of the four emperors', as different army commanders tried to seize power. First was Galba, who refused to make the traditional gift of money to the Praetorian Guard and was assassinated in the Forum. Next came Otho, who committed suicide when his army was defeated by Vitellius. Finally Vitellius, in his turn, was defeated by the army commanded by Vespasian, dragged to the Forum and murdered. The civil war cost forty million sesterces and left the Empire in chaos. Government by civilian emperors had failed, and the Senate (which had supported all four claimants in turn) was a laughing-stock.

Titus Flavius Vespasian, who became emperor in December 69, made the Empire into a military dictatorship. He worked hard, rising before dawn. He even tried to get up from his deathbed, saying: 'An emperor should die on his feet.' During his reign the wild parties and excesses of the previous reigns came to an end. Vespasian reorganized the army and conquered new territory in Germany and northern Britain. The Jewish revolt was defeated and Masada, the last Jewish stronghold, was taken in AD 73. When the Romans entered the fortress they found that all the defenders, except two women and five children, had committed suicide.

In AD 79 Vespasian fell ill with the fever which caused his death. 'Oh dear, I think I'm turning into a god,' he joked.

He was succeeded by his son, Titus (AD 79-81), 'the darling of the human race', whose declared ambition was to help someone every day. During his reign Mount Vesuvius erupted, destroying and preserving the small town of Pompeii (see page 62). His last words were: 'I have only done one thing wrong,' but nobody could think what it might have been.

Titus was followed by his younger brother Domitian, who was possibly the cruellest and most brutal emperor of all. He was murdered by an ex-slave in AD 96.

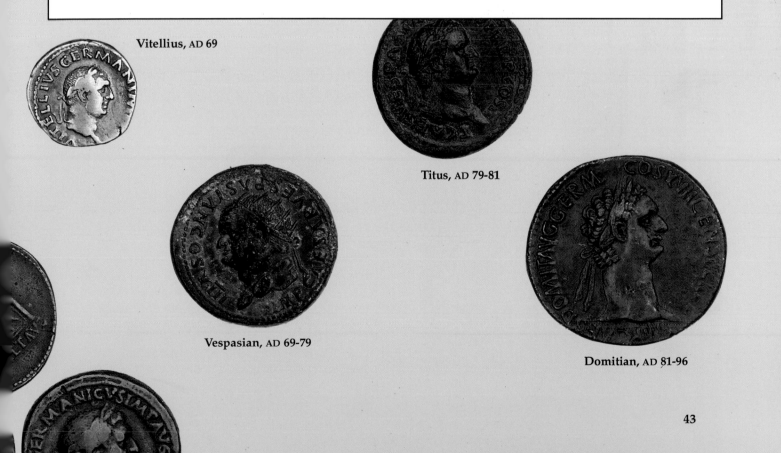

Vitellius, AD 69

Titus, AD 79-81

Vespasian, AD 69-79

Domitian, AD 81-96

Bread and Circuses

All the emperors realized that to stay in power they had to keep the plebeians fed and entertained. They gave them the *annona*, a monthly handout of free grain (there were riots if these supplies were late). They also presented entertainments such as athletics meetings, chariot races, gladiator contests and theatrical plays.

Nothing was spared to present a magnificent spectacle. Each day at the Greatest Games held by Nero, the Emperor gave away one thousand birds, food, money, slaves, houses and farms. In one play the actor playing Icarus actually tried to fly and crashed to his death, spattering the Emperor with blood – the Romans loved realism.

In the Greatest Games, Nero would not allow anyone to be killed, but this was not typical. Every year, thousands of criminals, slaves and prisoners of war were made to fight until only one of the day's combatants survived, or were put into the arena with wild animals. Innumerable animals, particularly elephants, were slaughtered. The politician Seneca was disgusted by the blood-lust of the games, especially as he found himself starting to enjoy the killing.

Chariot races were held at the Circus Maximus, Rome's grandest racetrack. Most other events were held in circular arenas (from the Latin *harena*, meaning 'sand') called amphitheatres. In AD 80, Titus opened the greatest amphitheatre of all, the Colosseum, which could seat fifty thousand spectators. To mark the occasion, games lasting one hundred days were held, at which nine thousand animals were killed.

At the games a *secutor* (swordsman) has overcome a *retiarius* (net-man) and the referee stops the fight. If the defeated man has fought well, the crowd will cheer and save his life. If he has fought badly, they will shout for him to die, and the official dressed as Charon, ferryman of the underworld, will club him to death. All gladiators, whatever weapons they use, are skilled fighters. Many survive long enough to buy their freedom. Some become famous stars and 'the idols of the young girls'.

Above left: a charioteer with one of his horses. The teams are named, from the colour of their shirts, the Reds, Whites, Blues and Greens. Chariot races are wild and dangerous. Afterwards, rival supporters attack each other. Fans put curses on their opponents, asking demons to 'torture and kill their horses and crush the drivers'.

Centre left: capturing animals for the games.

Left: loading ostriches onto a ship.

Rebuilding Rome

'The majesty of the Empire', wrote the architect Vitruvius in 27 BC, 'is shown in the magnificence of its public buildings.'

Augustus had boasted that he 'found Rome built of bricks and left her covered in marble'. He built the Temple of Mars to dominate the Forum, and the Temple of Jupiter on the Capitoline Hill overlooking Rome. He gave the Temple of Jupiter seven tons of gold, and jewels worth fifty million sesterces.

After the Great Fire of Rome in AD 64, Nero built on an even greater scale. His Golden House had walls covered with gold and jewels, ceilings made of ivory, gardens with a walkway 1 mile (1.6 kilometres) long, a huge dining-room with a revolving roof, and an entrance room with a statue of the Emperor 37 metres (120 feet) high.

During the reign of Vespasian, the building continued. The new emperor started the Colosseum, which required 400,000 tons of stone (greater than the weight of the Empire State Building in the United States). Titus continued these public works, building the Arch of Titus to commemorate the defeat of the Jewish revolt in AD 73 (see page 43).

Rome, the 'goddess of the earth', amazes visitors. The Romans are outstanding engineers, using cranes (above) to construct their great buildings.

Many buildings are covered in gold and marble. Interiors are decorated with mosaics made from small cubes of stone called *tesserae* – limestone for white and blue, brick or tile for red and purple, glass and ceramics for other colours.

Visitors coming to Rome (below) from southern Italy travel along the Appian Way (1) until they reach the Circus Maximus, the racetrack (2). Turning north, they go under the huge Aqua Claudia aqueduct (3) towards the Colosseum (4). Then they turn west along the Via Sacra, the Holy Road (5), past the Temple of Venus (6) and through the Arch of Titus (7) into the Forum Romanum (8). Open-mouthed, they look up towards the magnificent Temple of Jupiter (9) on the Capitoline Hill and know that they are standing at the centre of the world.

Aqueducts and Sewers

The Romans believed that polluted water and 'the smell of excrement' caused disease. As a result, they developed a system of aqueducts and sewers to keep the people healthy.

In the first century AD, nine aqueducts carried 222 million gallons (1,000 million litres) of water a day into Rome from lakes and streams in the surrounding hills. The scale was vast: the Aqua Claudia, built by the Emperor Claudius, was more than 40 miles (64 kilometres) long, used 600,000 tons of lime-stone in its construction and cost 30 million sesterces. The system, which included siphons, tunnels, filter tanks and arched bridges, was a marvel of hydraulic engineering. A team of 460 slaves maintained and repaired the aqueducts. Anyone obstructing the flow of water could be fined ten thousand sesterces, which shows its importance to the Romans.

An even greater achievement than the aqueducts, claimed the Roman writer Pliny, were the seven underground sewers. Streams flowed through tunnels large enough for a sailing boat, washing the city's sewage into the Cloaca Maxima, the main sewer, and

then on into the River Tiber.

Rome had a large number of public latrines. Each contained as many as 60 seats. Here, in full view of everybody else, the Romans sat and chatted, catching up on the latest gossip. Everyone had a sponge (used like paper today), which was rinsed in a channel of running water in the centre of the floor.

Arched bridges, such as the Pont du Gard in France, carry the aqueduct across valleys.

In Rome, most water goes to the temples and army barracks, and to the 591 cisterns and fountains from which most people take their water. About a third of

the water goes in lead pipes to private houses (above), although only the rich have running water. Householders pay for the amount of water they use.

Roman Roads

The Roman roads held the Empire together. They were its communication network, a key to its success and survival. They were so well constructed that after the Empire had collapsed (see page 60) legends grew up that they were the work of gnomes or giants.

The roads were used by a great variety of people: traders; mail couriers of the *cursus publicus* (a kind of pony express); government curators, off to check the financial accounts of a province; the proconsuls, collecting taxes; Christian missionaries, spreading the gospel; athletes, travelling from one race meeting to another; thousands of Roman citizens coming to Rome from all over the Empire to see the sights, or to put their case before the emperor; and by the legions, off to quell unrest in the provinces.

Few Romans enjoyed travelling, and most were homesick for Rome. Government officials could force local people to carry their baggage, but journeys were exhausting and people often died as a result of accidents, illnesses, or attacks by robbers. Inns were smoky, dirty and terrible firetraps. However, a traveller could have his wagon repaired, get a bed for the night and some wine, and perhaps flirt with the local girls.

The Peutinger Table is a medieval copy of a Roman map of the Empire's roads, giving distances between towns and the accommodation available. The top section shows the Balkans, the middle section shows Italy with Rome to the right, and Africa is at the bottom. More than 50,000 miles (80,450 kilometres) of roads cover the Empire at its greatest extent in AD 114 (see map, below).

Roads are built by the army. The surveyors plot a straight course from one landmark to the next. The engineers construct a strong base of logs and stones, then build up layers of different-sized stones, concrete, broken tiles, mud and sand, to create a well-drained, hard-wearing surface. In towns, roads such as this one in Ostia (left) are covered with large, smooth stones. At 100,000 sesterces per mile, the cost of road-building is so enormous that it has to be paid by the emperors.

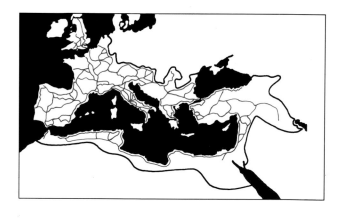

Gardellaca · XIII · Lusomana · XII · Aquinco · XIIII · Vetusallo · XII · Annamatia · XV · Lussonie · X · Altaripa

·o· VIII · Sonista · XII · puteis · XI · luntulis · VII · Iouia · X · Suttoris · X · Bolentio · IX · Marinnamē · VIII · Serontis · Ad pretor

A · quadrata · XIIII · Pad fines · XV · Sisera · Burnomilia · XII

Hadre a Bacauae · XII · Aserie · O · VI

XIII · Hedino · Sartlona · V

IIII · XV

Polentia · Milio · Sacrina · Fluor Ā · Tinna · Firmu Pirmu · Castello Firmani · Cupru Martina · Castro trenino · Castro

firmo vicerio · X · Cisternas · III · Cirulos · XII · Pirnum · XII · Prisserio · XII · interamnos

Surpicano · XV · interocrio · Aque cutilie · Reate · Ad nouas · Homento · VIII · Tibo

Ad martis · Palsernis · forocer · VII · VII · VIII · XVI · Cicto · XII · Fidenis · via salar · Ā · Aquar

inter manana · VII · via Humana nilia · Varubur · via nentana

Idine Recine · XI · literamnia · XI · Aequo falisco · XVI · Farfar · Aqua uiua · Ad uicesimu · Ā · Arubini · VI · Ad ponte tolu · Roma · via nentana

VIII · Vetos · VII · Ad sertim · via clodia · fonte adrian salis · via laticana

Careias · VIII · co uariat · via latina

II · Turres · Bebiana · Iorio · XII · via aurelia · via appia

VI · Pyrgos · X · Alsium · VI · VIII · via Hostensis · Hostis

Gallum Gallinacium · XV · Ittatragur colon · Thun

XVI · Tuiuburbimmus · III · Thuraria · XV · cicila · XVIII · Ad mercurium · IIII · Ad pertusa · VIII

IIII · Sicilibba · XII · Inuca · II · XV · Onellana · XII · Urtica

VI · VERIS · X · Aurta · VIII · Tuburbomaus · XV · XI · Bibae

Risca · XVIII · Anula · VII · Auripistara · VI · Vicopa

XVIII · Tuasarte · Athasartho · silosu muta · P

Thuges · X · va · Thusuros

The Height of Empire

After the short reign of the Emperor Nerva (AD 96-98), Trajan came to power. He was a Spaniard – the first emperor to come from a provincial family. During his reign (AD 98-117) the Roman Empire reached its greatest extent (see map, page 50).

In AD 105-106, Trajan conquered Dacia with an army of perhaps 120,000 legionaries. A huge concrete and stone monument, 30 metres (100 feet) in diameter and dedicated to Mars the Avenger, still stands in Romania, commemorating the campaign.

Returning to Rome, Trajan organized 117 days of games to celebrate his victory. He built a new forum, including two libraries, more than 150 shops and offices, and Trajan's Column. He constructed a new aqueduct and a huge new bathhouse. To please the plebeians, he increased the *annona* and added a new welfare benefit, the *alimenta* (to support poor children).

In AD 114 Trajan invaded Armenia, and the next year conquered the Persian Empire. He was the first – and the last – Roman general to see the Persian Gulf. It was impossible for one man to hold together such a huge empire. In AD 116 there were rebellions in Persia. In the same year Jews throughout the Empire rose in revolt. Trajan set out to return to Rome but died from a stroke on the way.

Trajan's soldiers attack and drive back Persian troops.
Above: some of the 155 scenes from the war against Dacia which are carved on Trajan's Column.

Exploiting the Provinces

For luxuries, the Romans depended on the huge empire that they had built up.

The army brought back plunder from its wars of conquest. According to his doctor, the Emperor Trajan, for instance, brought back from his Dacian wars hundreds of tons of gold and silver, herds of horses and fifty thousand slaves.

The provinces also provided taxes. Some were paid in money, but most were sent to Rome as goods (see page 20). Each province had to support the legions stationed there. Governors and tax collectors were not paid; they took as their wages any extra money they could squeeze from the inhabitants. Becoming a governor was seen as a way to get rich quickly. 'Spare a thought for the poor locals – you'll find they've already been bled dry,' the poet Juvenal advised new governors.

Some historians claim that heavy taxation damaged the local economies and caused a drop in world population which led to the fall of the Roman Empire.

To provide animals for the games, lions and elephants were wiped out in northern Africa and the Middle East. Forest-clearance in northern Africa reduced the rainfall, destroyed the soil, and turned vast areas into desert.

'The Romans have exhausted the land by their plunder. Robbery, butchery…they create a wasteland, and call it peace,' the British chieftain Calgacus was said to have complained. It is interesting that the words were put into his mouth years later by the Roman historian Tacitus, writing in about AD 100. Perhaps the Romans felt guilty.

Collecting taxes in Britain. A centurion records the amount of grain being handed over by a farmer. Britain supplies Rome with corn, cattle, hunting dogs, bears, pearls, silver, lead, tin, salt, wool and pottery.

Governing the Provinces

Each province of the Empire was ruled by a Roman governor, who quelled riots and judged legal cases such as forgery, robbery and rape, which carried the death penalty. Wherever possible, the Romans used the people who had been in control before the conquest to look after local government matters such as roads, markets, temples and the water supply. They allowed each race to keep its own customs and religions, insisting only that they also worshipped the emperor, which for Romans was not a religious matter but a test of loyalty. This explains the constant trouble between the Romans and the Jews, who refused to worship any god but Yahweh.

All Romans believed that they were bringing civilization to a world of barbarians. 'The Romans', claimed the Greek writer Aristides, 'have spanned rivers with bridges, cut through mountains to make roads, filled lonely places with farmsteads, and made life easier by supplying its needs and enforcing law and order. The whole world is as trim as a garden…It is as if the world had been ill, but has been made healthy.'

In practice, however, Roman rule was ruthless and often cruel. The Romans followed the principle of 'divide and rule' – legionaries recruited in one part of the Empire were sent to other provinces to keep order amongst people they despised. One governor in Asia executed three hundred men in a single day and strolled among the corpses exclaiming: 'What a royal deed!'

The Romans encourage the natives to develop towns, offering financial help to build temples and a forum. Gradually, the provincials start to wear Roman clothes and copy Roman manners.

In very backward areas such as Britain and Numidia, where Trajan built a huge settlement at Thamugadi in AD 100, they establish colonies (cities of ex-soldiers) to serve as an example of the civilized Roman way of life for the local inhabitants to follow.

Romanization

For the peasants in the provinces, life under the Romans continued exactly as it always had. Throughout the Empire, however, wealthy provincials adopted Roman ways. They went to the games, built public bathhouses and theatres, and installed central heating. In Syria, Muttumbal, son of Auchusor, started calling himself Muttumbalius Auchusorius, learned Latin and began to wear a toga. Africans built Roman-style villas and decorated them with paintings and mosaics. In Northumberland in England, a British farmer left his thatched Iron Age hut and moved with his family into a villa he had built next door. Archaeological evidence suggests that his mother, more set in her ways, stayed behind.

In the later years of the Empire, thousands of provincials were allowed to buy Roman citizenship. Like St Paul in the Bible, they were able to say proudly *'Civis Romanus sum'* ('I am a Roman citizen'). If they were accused of a crime, they could go to Rome to appeal directly to the emperor to decide their case. The richest provincials became senators and travelled to Rome to attend the Senate.

The people of the Empire were 'tempted to

become peaceful'. Nobody wanted to serve in the army, and the government relied increasingly on the peoples from the outlying provinces and beyond – Germans, Britons and Syrians. The Syrians, mutinous and disobedient, left their posts, got drunk and regarded the trumpet blast 'as a signal not for advance, but for retreat'.

The Roman villa system is introduced as the basis of agriculture in many provinces of the Empire. A villa (right) is not just a manor house, but a complex of buildings. For the landowner there are living-rooms with underfloor heating, wall paintings, colourful mosaics, and a private bathhouse. There may also be a farmhouse for the labourers, a prison for the slaves, stables, cowsheds, storehouses, granaries with raised floors to keep out the rats, and rooms for wine and olive presses.

The olive crop is gathered in December. Long sticks are used to beat the olives from the branches.

Decline and Fall

After Trajan's death the Emperor Hadrian (AD 117-138) realized that if the Empire grew any larger it would become ungovernable. He concentrated instead on defending the frontiers. He travelled constantly through the Empire, reviewing the troops and building forts and defences.

Once the Empire stopped growing, however, it began to decline. The government became paralysed by corruption and intrigue. Between AD 138 and 361, 30 out of 42 emperors were murdered, or killed in battle. Faced with the constant threat of assassination, many emperors either lived scandalously or became vicious tyrants. The death of the emperor was often the signal for an armed struggle between army generals.

Robbers and pirates disrupted trade routes. The northern frontier of the Empire was attacked by terrifying barbarian tribesmen. The Roman writer Ammianus reported with horror that one of these tribes, the Huns, ate raw flesh, warming it only between their legs and the backs of their horses. 'They dress in the skins of fieldmice sewn together. They are almost glued to their horses and relieve themselves in that position,' he wrote.

In AD 330 the Emperor Constantine moved the capital of the Empire to Constantinople (Istanbul). The Empire was divided into two, and had two emperors. In Constantinople the laws and culture of Rome were kept safe for more than a thousand years. Rome itself, however, was unable to resist invasion. In AD 410 the Goths plundered the city, and in 476 the last emperor in Rome was deposed. Western Europe entered the Dark Ages, when law, learning and city life disappeared.

Roman soldiers guard one of the forts along Hadrian's Wall in Britain. Stretching 72 miles (116 kilometres) across the north of England, it has been built to try to keep out the Picts, tribesmen who live in Scotland.

How Do We Know?

There are many written sources available to historians, who can read the opinions of Roman politicians, generals and travellers. Writers such as Juvenal and Martial produced short, witty descriptions of everyday life (see, for example, page 23). Modern historians can read about the events of Roman history as they were seen by Roman historians such as Tacitus and Suetonius (see pages 38-39).

These texts have to be used carefully. The writings of Juvenal and Martial are exciting, but the historian must remember that they exaggerated the problems of life to make people laugh.

It is also important to realize that Roman historians generally opposed the emperors, and it is difficult to establish what truth lies behind their hostile accounts. Tacitus openly admitted that he let his opinions influence his writing: 'It is an historian's duty to praise the good things and to speak out against evil deeds and words.'

Ruins and Remains

The Romans were excellent engineers and many of their buildings and monuments, made of stone and concrete, still stand. In Rome the visitor can see the remains of the Forum Romanum (see page 24), the Colosseum and the Arch of Titus (see page 46). The relief carvings on Trajan's Column (see page 53) have been a major source for historians of the Roman Army, and are one of the few sources we have for Trajan's Dacian Wars. If you go to Nîmes, in France, you can still see the Pont du Gard aqueduct (see page 49), visit a Roman amphitheatre, or walk into a Roman temple (the Maison Carrée, see above right). At Timgad in Algeria (the Roman Thamugadi, see page 56), you can see the well-preserved

ruins of a complete Roman city. In the north of England, historians can walk along the remains of Hadrian's Wall (see page 60) and imagine they are Roman soldiers watching for the Picts.

In the nineteenth century, the Italian archaeologist Guiseppe Fiorelli began excavating the most remarkable site of all – the town of Pompeii, buried under a mountain of ash when Mount Vesuvius erupted. Everything was preserved exactly as it was at the moment when life in Pompeii stopped, in the early afternoon of 24 August AD 79. On the

ground floor of one *insula*, in the bar which belonged to Asellina (her name is painted on the wall), excavators found the water that was being heated in the kettle, 18 centuries earlier. Where people had been buried by the eruption, cavities had been left as their bodies decayed. Fiorelli invented a method of pouring plaster into the holes to make casts of the bodies in the positions they were in at the moment of death: a girl hiding her face in her father's clothes; a family fleeing down the street, the children falling first, then the mother, and finally the father, overcome by the ash and fumes.

In addition to these and other archaeological sites and artefacts, there are thousands of inscriptions (telling us about the careers of the people they commemorate), as well as mosaics, wall paintings and graffiti, which give us an insight into the everyday lives of the Romans. Roman coins are so numerous that they are quite cheap to buy; they are important to the historian because the inscriptions and pictures on them were used as propaganda by the emperors, and reveal what they wanted people to believe.

The Renaissance and Roman Culture

From the second half of the fifteenth century, the Renaissance (rebirth) sparked off interest in Roman civilization, especially after the capture of the city of Constantinople by the Turks in 1453, when a large number of Latin documents were taken back to western Europe. In Italy, Pope Clement XIV (1769-1774) founded the Vatican Museum and collected Roman remains. In England and France architects copied the Roman style of building. This became known as the classical style, because it was considered to be without equal. A study of Latin texts ('classics') and a

'grand tour' of Italy were an essential part of the education of wealthy young Englishmen in the eighteenth century.

Between 1776 and 1788 one of these young men, Edward Gibbon, published his book, *The Decline and Fall of the Roman Empire*. The book was an epic, describing a Roman Empire sinking under the 'slow and secret poison' of tyranny and decadence, until 'the fierce giants of the north broke in and restored a manly spirit of freedom'. Gibbon has influenced historians of the Roman Empire ever since. Until recently, all history undergraduates at Oxford University in England began their first term with a study of *The Decline and Fall*, to see how history should be written.

The Past in the Present

Roman civilization has survived in another, less obvious way, passed down through the ages in the developing traditions, institutions and attitudes of the western world (see page 6). During the time of the Roman Empire, a fish sauce called *garum* became popular all over Europe and even further afield. In India it continued to be used until the nineteenth century, when government officials of the British Empire rediscovered it and brought the recipe back to England, where it is now sold as Worcester sauce.

A great deal has changed beyond recognition over the years. Where Roman traditions still survive, they have often lost their original meaning. Newly-wed husbands still carry their wives across the threshold, but no longer to demonstrate their control over the household. Despite the changes, however, Rome provided the foundation on which modern civilization was built. There is a little of the Roman in all of us.

At Pompeii, the plaster cast of a girl (left) conveys the sadness of the disaster. Stepping stones in the street (far left) prevented feet from getting muddy.

Index